Tumbling And Trampoline In Amarillo Texas

```
I0161103
```

by

Pat Hamilton

ISBN-10:0692156577
ISBN-13:9780692156575

DEDICATION

I dedicate this book to the memory of Ralph Dykeman and the Maverick Boys Club..

Without the Maverick Club my life would not have been as exciting.
I also want to dedicate this project to my daughter Mandi and granddaughters Kaitlyn and Shaylee for giving me the opportunity to coach into my old age.
Mandi Placed fifth in the National Age Group Championships on Double Mini Tramp while at Gymagic in Victoria Texas.

This project is a labor of love for the people I have met and the kids I have taught in the Sports of Gymnastics, Trampoline and Tumbling.

This history had to be written down before it was lost. It may contain mistakes but they are honest ones. Please forgive me if I left anything out

Check out the Youtube Video on the Maverick Club

Maverick Club Tumbling the Old Days

You just might see yourself there!

The New Maverick Club opened in 1950
This is the location today at 1923 S. Lincoln

National T&T Championships 2016 Fort Worth, Texas

LR: Pat Hamilton-Tim Hall-Tex Womack-Steve Elliott- Jerry Strickland

Table of Contents

Nards in Wolflin Village when it first opened in 1959

ACKNOWLEDGMENTS

I would like to thank the following for helping me gather information for this project:

Ron Munn

Dagmar (Nissen) Munn

David Jacobs

Linda Shepard

Glenn Hedrick

Tim Hall

Beverly Hamilton

Jerry Strickland

Patty Taylor Crockett

Mandi Gonzales

Nard's 1959

CHAPTER 1
INTRODUCTION

I was blessed to enter this world on May 11, 1950 as a post war "Baby Boomer". My parents had survived the Dust Bowl, the Great Depression and WWII.

My dad was hard drinking and hard working. He taught us how to be tough and to take care of ourselves. Mom dutifully hauled us all to Church every Sunday and taught us to be Godly people.

We were poor but didn't know it because everyone we knew lived just likes us. I don't remember much about my early years except when we got our first TV. That was 1956 the year I entered the first grade.

I grew up in a town most people considered the coldest wind blown place on the planet. I grew up in the "Pride of the Golden Spread", The Tri State Jewel of Amarillo, Texas.

To most, Amarillo was a sleepy and boring backwater of a town. To me it was exciting and hard but never boring. The memories of Amarillo feel like an old shoe, like grandma's quilt. I get warm and fuzzy thinking about the wonderful times I had when I was growing up.

Amarillo was located on the Santa Fe and Topeka Railway line. People toiled on the land, worked in the oil patch or labored in various manufacturing, ranching or merchandising efforts.

Right after the Dust Bowl and the Great Depression, Amarillo was growing rapidly and for the most part kids just took care of themselves. Many young boys had nothing special to do and boys being boys usually found something to tear up or some kind of mischief to get into. The leaders of Amarillo saw a need to get these boys off the street and into something constructive.

One day over coffee in 1934, Chanslor E. Weymouth, Cal Farley, and Roy Pool agreed that a boys club was the answer to the problems of unsupervised leisure of the boys in Amarillo. With $300 each and a building donated by Mary E. Bivins, they put together a club for the boys to go to. They named it the Maverick Boys Club. The name "Maverick" is a word used by the old cowboys for an unbranded calf that was loose and roaming the prairie.

Ralph Dykeman, a strong athletic young man, was visiting Amarillo. Ralph was a wrestler and knew a lot of acrobatic skills and how to build human pyramids. Ralph had spent time at Muscle Beach in California. He got to know Cal and Dutch Mantell while wrestling. (Ralph was also the Uncle to Debbie Reynolds, the famous Hollywood actress.)

Cal asked Ralph if he would help get the boys off the street and help start the club. Ralph agreed to stay a little while to help out. He finally retired in 1984 after dedicating his life to helping these young boys. There have been thousands perhaps tens of thousands of boys and girls from Amarillo that have benefited from that meeting over coffee in 1934 and from Ralph Dykeman, the greatest man I've ever known.

The first Club was located at 313 Van Buren Street. This is the where my dad and my Uncle John joined the Maverick club. They were original Mavericks. I took great pride every time Mr. Dykeman introduced me as a Second Generation "Maverick." There wasn't even a paved road in front of the club and the boys would spend Saturdays picking up nails off the ground so they could play in the dirt.

In 1936, the Club moved to the old Amarillo College. Later Mary Bivins donated land and a building at 3rd and Grant. Everyone called this the "Old Club." The Old Club offered a place for the boys to go. This building was right behind Cal's Farley's Gas and Service Station.

Mr. Dykeman taught the boys how to box, wrestle, lift weights and how to tumble. Along with tumbling Mr. Dykeman taught the boys how to do a lot of different pyramids and stunts.

The Maverick Club did its job and offered a place for the boys to go. Many times these boys broke the rules and there was always a consequence for doing that. Everyone was required to say "Yes sir"No sir, Thank you sir, etc." Ralph taught the boys respect and manners. When the boys broke a serious rule they received swats. We would bend over and Mr. Dykeman would dish out 5, 10 or 15 swats. After the swats our name was placed on the paddle with a mark for each 5 swats you received. It became a matter of pride on how many lines on the various paddles you had marked.

Mr. Dykeman had the perfect motivational system. You received a challenge on doing a new skill. If you completed the skill, you got a coke. If you missed, it was five swats for you. We were poor so we'd risk everything for a coke. Motivation was either positive or negative but it was just and swift and hard.

Many times the boys would be scraggly and dirty. Ralph would make sure his boys were washed up and he even cut their hair when needed. He taught us all how to be men and how to act right. Mr. Dykeman knew something about chiropractic methods. He learned them while at Muscle Beach in California. Many times my dad and other men would come in for a back adjustment. He would lay them down on the wooden bowling table and pop their backs. He would hold grown men up with their arms crossed and pop their backs. It was really scary watching him pop the necks. He would slowly move the head around with his hands on the cheeks and then pop the head quickly and you would hear the "crack" of the neck. He just knew everything about all things. He was a true model and hero for us wayward boys.

The first Mavericks learned to tumble. The first mats were army cot mattresses sewn together and covered by a canvas. These were supplied by army surplus from the Amarillo Air Force Base located on the edge of town. Everything we had came from army surplus. Buses, jeeps, bedrolls, tents, and tools were received from the Amarillo Air force Base. Our first trampoline was a solid canvas bed with shock cords". If we needed it and the army had it we got it. I thought normal color was fatigue green until I was fifteen.

The Maverick colors were red and white. I guess it was to offset that army green we had everywhere. We painted the buses and jeeps and everything we could red and white. To this day I love the colors red and white and being a Maverick.

Some of the first Mavericks were John and Bill Hamilton, John Cobb Jr., Bobby Boyter, Hester Plant, Ed and Donnie Sharp, Fred, Roy and Gene Turner and JC Oakley. Bill was my dad and John (Red) Hamilton was my uncle. These first Mavericks learned to tumble and build pyramids. Mr. Dykeman taught them many tricks and actions of circus performers. These boys would travel the panhandle doing shows and exhibitions for the public. The Club was supported by donations from the public and donations and help from Cal Farley, Dutch Mantel, The Bivins family and many others that wanted the boys to do well.

After WWII a discharged paratrooper returned to Amarillo. He had seen paratroopers use a new bouncing device to practice landings. He used these new devices and loved them and the feeling of falling and bouncing. This man was Benard Cazzell. We all just called him "Nard".

Nard would drop by the Maverick Club and help Mr. Dykeman and the boys from time to time. He managed to purchase one of these new devices used in the Army training. George Nissen and Larry Griswald had invented and modified this device to what it is today. It's called a trampoline. Nard became the trampoline coach for the Mavericks.

In 1946 Ralph and Nard trained the boys of the Club to bounce on the trampoline and do all sorts of tricks. Ralph concentrated on the tumbling and Nard took control of the trampoline. By this time my dad and Uncle John had served in WWII and were out starting families.

Even though my Uncle John was grown and making a living with the railroad he continued working and helping at the Club his entire life. His son Johnny became one of the most outstanding tumblers and trampoliners to ever come out the Club. He won the Big Ten Championships in trampoline while on full scholarship at the University of Michigan and placed second in the NCAA Championships in 1964. Johnny also placed fourth in the World Professional Trampoline Championships in 1964. This action by my Uncle John and cousin Johnny had a profound impact on my life and set me on the trampoline and tumbling path and helped me get full athletic scholarships at Odessa College and LSU New Orleans.

Two of the first trampoliners were Edsel Buchannan and Jack Tillinghast. Edsel won three straight NCAA Championships while at Michigan University and Jack Tillinghast helped at the Club, and later with Nard Cazzell while introducing trampoline as a Professional Educator at West Texas State University.

In the early 70's Jack Tillinghast held the National AAU Trampoline Championships at West Texas State University. He purchased a lot of the trampolines for WT. Later Jerry Strickland and I helped teach trampoline for him at West Texas State.

Dr. Edsel Buchannan went on to be a professor of Physical Education at Texas Tech University. As Mavericks we did many, many exhibitions at Tech and at WT for football and basketball games for halftime shows.

After starting trampoline at the Club and helping train the boys Nard decided to branch out and open his own trampoline place out in an old lakebed that's now called Wolflin Village. By the time I started in 1956 there was a strong rivalry between Nard and the Maverick Club.

Some of the boys Nard and Mr. Dykeman worked with in those early days were Robert Elliott, Ron Munn, Tim Joe Way and Richard McFarland. Tim Joe married Nard's daughter, Vicki. Richard's sister went on to marry Robert Elliott. (Out of this marriage came two outstanding athletes in the form of Steve and Scott Elliott.)

When Nard opened his facility Tim and Richard went with him but Robert stayed at the Maverick Club. Nards had both boys and girls. One of the outstanding girls was Ann Bynum Whittenburg . Ann later competed at the National AAU Championships in Kingspoint Long Island. Kenny Vineyard from the Maverick Club competed at that same Championship.

Robert Elliott went to Florida State University and won the USA and Canadian National Championships on Trampoline. Tim Joe went to Iowa and he and Richard McFarland won many Southwest AAU Championships and competed in the first World Professional Trampoline Championships sponsored by George Nissen. Both were finalist at the competition.

When I started in 1956, had we heard about Bobby Boyter, Edsel Bucanhan, Jack Tillinghast, Robert Elliott, Tim Joe Way, and Richard McFarland. Active Champions at the time were Ron Munn, Johnny Hamilton, Tommy Russ, Phillip Garcia and Anthony Gallegos.

Ron Munn, Johnny Hamilton, Tim Joe and Richard McFarland went on to achieve much bigger things in gymnastics and the others faded as they left high school. Then came Kenny Vinyard and David Jacobs. David became World Champion. (More on David later.) Kenny Vinyard competed nationally in trampoline. He also became an outstanding place kicker and became an All-American football player at Texas Tech. He was drafted by Green Bay and played for Atlanta. Kenny was inducted into the Texas Tech Hall of Fame for football.

After football Kenny came back to the Maverick Club and learned to coach from Johnny Hamilton. Johnny returned to the Club to work and finish up his teaching certificate at West Texas A&M. Both Kenny and Johnny became outstanding coaches in gymnastics and opened their own private clubs.

Athletes in my generation were Johnny Plant, Odess Lovin, Johnny

Cobb, Richard Womack (Tex) Roy Smith, Tay and Bruce Carter, Ronnie Webb, Roger Hudson, George Dodgen, Billy Bob Taylor, Tim Hall, Scott Elliott, Steve Elliott and Gary Hedrick. From Nard's you had Jerry Strickland, Vance Hall, Linda Shepard, Kathy Dodgen, Steve McFarland, Chad Fox, Cliffie Lewellan, Kip Frazier and Shannon Bennett

I loved my time at the Maverick Club and miss the friendships and fun we all had. I'm writing this book to make sure it is not lost to history. So many Champions from such a small town is truly extraordinary and a great accomplishment for my hometown. I can't imagine any other town in the World that had as many champions as Amarillo has had in Tumbling and Trampoline.

I will describe the players in Tumbling, Trampoline and gymnastics the best I can. Much of what will be written will come from memory. If there are mistakes, wrong dates or someone left out I will apologize in advance. I will try and place these individuals in order and tell you as much as I can about their achievements. Starting with the most important one who without his help none of this would have ever happened. Ralph Dykeman my hero and the best man I have ever known.

The first Maverick Tumblers were: Donnie Sharp, Myron Brewer, Glen McDowell, Fulton Shepard, I. W. Clark, Ed Sharp, Lee Roy Boyter, W.C. Evans, Grady Rutledge, Bill Bailey, J,C. Oakley, Alvis Grant, Artie Brewer, G.C. Clark, John Hamilton, John Cobb, Hester Plant, R.A. Boyer, Marlin Sharp, Billy Floyd and Wesley Grier.

Members of the World Acrobatic Society Hall of Fame

From Amarillo

Ron Munn	David Jacobs
Edsel Buchanan	Nard Cazzell
Jon Beck	Steve McFarland
Steve Elliott	Tim Hall

CHAPTER 2
Ralph Dykeman

Ralph Dykeman was the pillar of the Maverick Boys Club in Amarillo from 1935 to 1976, a forty-two year coaching career. He was one of the early great figures in the growth of Texas gymnastics. Mr. Dykeman's first major competition with his athletes came at the AAU meet in Dallas in 1947, with Charlie Pond as the Meet Director. The Mavericks, wearing red shoes, were tumbling, trampoline and later mini-tramp specialists.

The list of Ralph's AAU champions began in 1946 with Bobby Hudgins, Eddie Tilley in 1947, Dale Hulsy in 1951, Joe Tim Way in 1952, Robert Elliott in 1952, 1953, 1954 and 1955. Elliott was National Senior Trampoline champion in 1954 and won tumbling and trampoline at the Southwestern AAU. Ralph Boynton won the Junior National Title in trampoline in 1954, followed by Johnny Hamilton, David Jacobs and Kenny Vinyard. The list continued in the 1960s with Tommy Russ, Richard Womack, Phil Garcia, Johnny Cobb, Johnny Plant, Ronnie Webb,

George Dodgen and Pat Hamilton all winning Junior or Senior
SWAAU trampoline or tumbling titles. A great Maverick team
won the Junior National AAU team title in 1968. Mr. Dykeman
became an Honorary Life Member of the Gymnastics Association
of Texas in 1969, the second person to be so honored in Texas. In
1978 he was elected to the National Trampoline Hall of Fame.

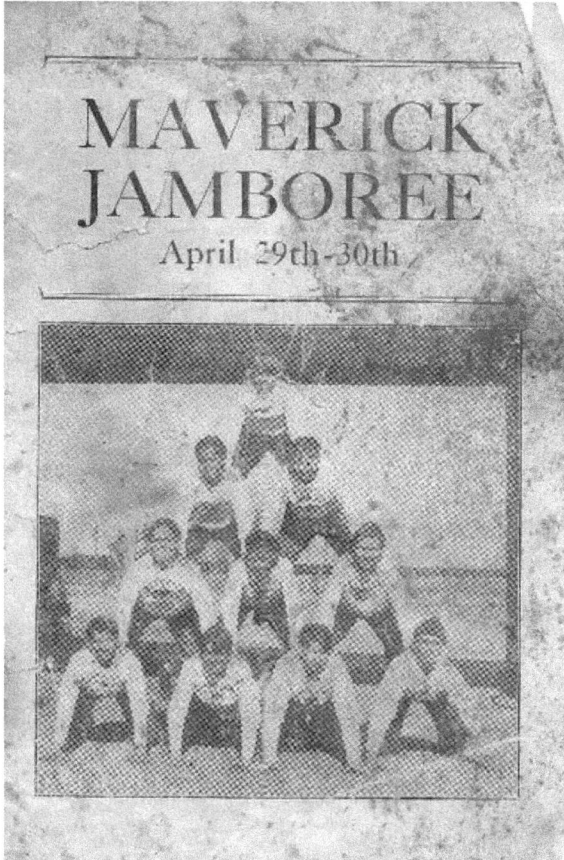

Maverick Pyramid Builders – The first Maverick tumblers

**Myran Brower, Gary Rutledge, Glen McDowell, Donnie Sharp,
Lidel Pugh, Artie Brewer, Drue Cole, Bunyan Lilley, Fred Turner,
Roy Turner, Jerald Hughes, Junior Keith, Bill Bailey, J.C Oakley,**

Oscar Robbins, Fulton Sheaperd, J.W. Clark, Gene Turner, Lee Roy Boyter, Alan Boarts, Ed sharp, Avis Grant, W.C. Evans, Joe Bob Floyd, John (Red) Hamilton, Hester Plant, R.A. Boyter, John Cobb, Photo: Gene Rutledge 1936

Maverick Gas Station 3rd and Grant

The Old Club

Maverick Handstands 1939

Maverick Tumblers 1939

Top L/R: Johnny Hamilton, Dale Pair, Ralph Dykeman, ?, Sherald Fenimore,

Bottom: Phillip Garcia, Benny Garcia, Kenny Vinyard, ?

Photos by Amarillo Globe News

STATE CHAMPIONS - TROPHYS WON HOUSTON DEC 28 1960

LR :Tommy Russ, David Jacobs, Kenny Vinyard, Phillip Garcia

LR: Roger Hudson, Pat Hamilton, Kenny Vineyard, Ralph Dykeman

George Dodgen, Richard Womack

Bottom Mike Holloway, Roy Smith, Odess Lovin

Nard Cazzell

From the Amarillo Globe News
Posted: Friday, May 19, 2000
Jon Mark Beilue, Amarillo Globe-News Sports Editor

Nard Cazzell was a father figure to countless number of Amarillo youth for generations through his work as a coach in gymnastics, swimming and diving and trampoline.

Nard was born in Amarillo in 1913 and graduated from Amarillo High School. After one year at Texas A&M University, he joined the Navy where he soon developed a love for trampoline and the art of twisting and turning, which he turned into his life's work. The Navy used trampolines in its aviation preflight training program, and Cazzell became hooked.

"I just fell in love with it because it was so much fun," Cazzell once said. "I had dived a lot when I was a kid so that probably had something to do with it."

After the Navy in 1946, Cazzell went back to Amarillo and purchased a trampoline and donated it to the Maverick Club. He began his teaching career with six students.

"I sent off for some books and started reading them," he said. "One was written by Larry Griswold. He was one of the first to write about trampoline. It was published in 1943. That book became my bible!"

Cazzell's career took off after that. In 1954, he and his wife, Sissie, opened Nard's Gymnastics School, which he operated for more than 30 years, teaching gymnastics and tumbling to area youngsters. The school has continued to operate at the same location, now the All-American Gymnastics owned by a Maverick, Tim Hall.

Many of his students went on to national acclaim. Ronnie Munn was a national champion at 15 and went on to become the President of the U.S. Trampoline Association. Dave Jacobs was a national collegiate champion at the University of Michigan, and Chad Fox was a multi-event NCAA gymnastics champion at the University of New Mexico in the 1990s. Chad is the only gymnast to win four NCAA Championships in a row. Chad accomplished this in Vaulting.

Cazzell had an engaging personality, a high-pitched squeaky voice and a unique ability to motivate athletes.

"He kind of adopted half the world as his kids," said his daughter, Vicki Nichols. "He loved the kids and did anything in the world for them."

The International Gymnastics Hall of Fame reference book, "Roots of American Gymnastics," lists Cazzell and some of his students as pioneers in its reference section titled "Texas Panhandle Gymnastics." Trampolining, which was influenced heavily by

Cazzell, will be a medal event for the first time at the 2000 Olympics in Sydney.

In 1994, the United State Gymnastics Federation honored him with the organization's lifetime achievement award. Cazzell was just the fifth person so honored by the national federation.

Cazzell was a member of the Gymnastics Association of Texas Hall of Fame, and was the 111th inductee into the Panhandle Sports Hall of Fame in 1997. He died at age 86 in September, 1999.

Posted on the

From the Gymnastics Association of Texas site:

Posthumously Inducted: 2002
Born: Amarillo, Texas

The Texas Gymnastics Association's highest award is the SPECIAL LIFE MEMBER AWARD. Nard Cazzell received the award in 1971 and is described by the group as ". . . one of the rich characters – and great coaches – who added so much to hundreds of trampoline and gymnastics championships over the years. Nard Cazzell was dedicated to the sport of gymnastics for over 40 years, yet with Nard, his athletes always came first."

Nard is a lifetime member of USA Trampoline and Tumbling and was recently inducted into the World Acrobatics Society Gallery of Honor, (2002). He grew up in Amarillo and attended Texas A&M University where he was an Olympic hopeful in swimming and diving. After serving in the U.S. Navy during WWII, he coached the sport of Trampoline at the Maverick Boy's Club in Amarillo.

Not only did some of his students do well nationally on the trampoline, some also became champion divers. Nard Cazzell is credited as being instrumental in designing the first competition trampoline with George Nissen. In his over 40 years of teaching boys and girls trampoline and gymnastics, Cazzell holds the record for the most national champions trained by one coach. He was also one of the founding fathers of the U.S. association of Independent Gymnastics Clubs (USAIGC) in the 1970's. Nard received the National Tumbling Coach of the Year and the national Trampoline Coach of the Year Awards, (1985). Once labeled a pioneer in the sport, Nard is considered a major factor in the acceptance of trampoline in the Olympics. He began coaching competitive trampoline in Amarillo, and produced 50 national champions in all three trampoline disciplines, (1980-'85). His impact on the many who learned from him and the development of trampolining in the U.S. and abroad strongly tells us that he was a man who changed life in the gym as well as productively changing life in the world for those in his charge as well as those who learned, were influenced, but never met him.

Sources: Thanks are due the Texas Gymnastics Association through their website www.gatx.org/awards.htm, plus the courtesy of Jerry Wright's photo and biographical information presented in his book *Gymnastics Who's Who, 2005*. Introduction, commentary, and formatting by Larry Banner, Web Manager

According to Ron Munn (early Nard athlete): "When I was in the 7th grade Nard Cazzell had started a small trampoline school for after school trampoline classes with two trampolines on the stage of the Amarillo Little Theater. As a promotion for his school and to drum up business he came to a 7th grade Valentines dance at Austin Junior High School and with two of his students gave an exhibition....finding out about his school I convinced my parents to let me sign up for lessons. Nard was my coach (teacher) all the way through high school until I attended the University of Michigan on a scholarship. At that time my competitive team members in Amarillo were Charles Rittenberry, Jo Tim Way, Johnnie Hersh, Bill O'Brien and Nards daughter Vicki. There were other students at the trampoline school as well, but these are the ones I remember competing with at meets around Texas.

Nard moved his school to a warehouse behind a drug store on Washington Street with a few more trampolines and from there in the summer of 1954 built the very first trampoline school in the U.S. which is still there today as you know. During these early years we competed against the Maverick Club, but since Robert Elliott was older I never competed against him. As a team we traveled to Fort Worth and Austin for Southwest A.A.U. meets.

Watch this Youtube video of Nard's.
Nards Trampoline Center 1954
https://www.youtube.com/watch?v=67bjPNQHRd

Chapter 3
Dr. Edsel Buchanan

NCAA Trampoline Champion 1949, 1950, 1951

National Trampoline Hall of Fame (1979)

Life Member Gymnastics Association of Texas (1981)

World Acrobatic Society Hall of Fame

Edsel was a graduate of Amarillo High School in (1946). As a member of the Amarillo Maverick Boys Club Edsel participated in the club's tumbling and trampoline program. As a result of the gymnastics training that he received from the Club and coach Ralph Dykeman and trampoline coach Nard Cazzell, Edsel received a gymnastics scholarship from the University of Michigan in 1948. As a gymnast at Michigan, Edsel won three consecutive NCAA trampoline championships (1949, 1950, 1951).

Although the Boys Club in Amarillo eventually had several collegiate gymnastics performers win a national trampoline championship. Edsel is the only one to win three consecutive championships in trampoline. Coaches for Edsel were: Newt

Loken at Michigan, Ralph Dykeman and Nard Cazzell.

Edsel was a cheerleader at Michigan as a student and was a cheerleader at a Rose Bowl game which Michigan won against the University of Southern California.

Edsel served as the National Intramural Association President and the NIA/NIRSA Executive Director. Edsel was the campus recreation director at Texas Tech for 25 years. Edsel earned a doctorate from the University of Houston with major interests in the administration of HPERD. Following two years at the University of North Texas, Edsel was hired in 1979 by the University of Nebraska at Omaha (UNO) as the chair of the academic program for Recreation and Leisure Studies.

Edsel did a lot of extra work helping the Maverick Boys Club. The Mavericks did many exhibitions of tumbling and trampoline at the half time of Texas Tech Basketball games.

Edsel saw military service during the Korean War along with two brothers, (my uncles) Jimmy and Kenneth Hamilton (KIA). There were many Maverick War heroes served during WWII, Korea and Vietnam.

Edsel at the 1949 NCAA Championships. He had to do a 31 bounce routine.

Watch this Youtube video of Edsel's 31 bounce routine:

https://www.youtube.com/watch?v=LLKsxGyg2GA

Jack Tillinghast

Life Member 1990 Gymnastics Association of Texas

As a young man, Jack Tillinghast grew up in Amarillo. There he fell under the spell of super-coach, Ralph Dykeman, and became a member of the Maverick Boys Club touring team. He learned tumbling and trampoline and proudly wore the red shoes of the Mavericks.

He competed in SWAAU, National and international tumbling and trampoline competition, and became a talented performer. With mentor Dykeman and fellow Maverick, Edsel Buchanan, then at Texas Tech, he was instrumental in creating the West Texas AAU association to provide competition for Panhandle and South Plains' athletes.

He and friend Buchanan formed an act called the "Flying Matadors," also in the 1950s. With this trampoline-tumbling-stunt show, they traveled the Panhandle area introducing tumbling, trampoline and gymnastics.

Since the 1950s, Tillinghast has been a member of the Physical Education Department at West Texas State University. He has taught dozens of the West Texas coaches during the years and has been a strong supporter of Nard Cazell's Sports/Acrobatic development in the 1980s, providing facilities at WTSU for competitions. He was the last of the Texas "pioneer generation" to be honored by the GAT Life Membership, with election in 1990.

Robert Elliott

NATIONAL A AU TRAMPOLINE CHAMPION
WON 1954 LOS ANGELES ROCHESTER N.Y 1955
WON CANADA TITLE 1954
ROBERT ELLIOTT

Robert Elliot, father of Steve E liot. His son followed the traditon.
National Meet trampoline champion 1954.

Robert was a Maverick that won the American and Canadian National championships in the early 50's. He married Richard McFarland's sister and they produced two outstanding athletes in Scott and Steve. (More about them later)

Robert attended Florida State University. FSU was a powerhouse of gymnastics in the 50's and 60's. Robert helped out at the Maverick Club from time to time and would offer valuable insight for me as I was learning to bounce.

Joe Tim Way/Richard McFarland

In 1964 Tim along with Richard McFarland competed in the first World Professional Trampoline Championships held in the Catskill Mountains in New York at the famous Grossinger's Hotel. Tim and Richard made the Finals in this competition.

Tim was a Maverick. Tim married Nard's daughter Vicki. Joe Tim was also a world renowned Judo/Aikido trainer and competitor.

Joe Tim was the owner and operator of the "Tim Joe's School of Judo/Aikido" and the Dolphin Swim Club from 1969 to 2008. Tim Joe attended the University of Iowa on a gymnastics scholarship

Richard was from Nard's Trampoline School and was an outstanding performer on the trampoline. His sister married Robert Elliott and solidified the family of Elliott and McFarland that produced Steve Elliott eight time world champion and Scott Elliott a major driving force in the Universal Cheerleading Association (UCA)

Ron Munn, Nard, Tim Joe

CHAPTER 4
RON MUNN

Ronnie Munn and the beginning of Nards

by Ron Munn

Meeting with and performing for King Hamad bin Isa al-Khalifa, Bahrain – 1977

"Attached are a few things that might be of help regarding my background over the years. In fact I found a trampoline in the yard across the street from Bivins Elementary School and decided to sneak in and bounce on it. That's how it started for me!

I should also point out that along with Eddie Cole we took the "Spaceball" game and made it into an act touring throughout the U.S. and parts of Europe."

Having worked 35 years for the Nissen Corporation as International Sales Manager I traveled throughout the world along with George Nissen.... the highlight was when we put the trampoline on top of the Great Pyramid in Egypt....here is the link to the entire "Caper."

www.hadtrampolinedidtravel.blogspot.com

"Ole Rebound Ron"

Ronnie started trampoline (no tumbling) on his own in someone's backyard across the street from Bivins Elementary School about 1951 or 52. They had purchased a trampoline and when they weren't home he'd jump the fence and bounce away and loved it! At that time he was in the 5th or 6th grade, so was he was about 11 or 12.

Ronnie began learning trampoline skills in that back yard on his own. When he was in the 7th grade Ron found out that Nard Cazell had started a small trampoline school for after school trampoline classes. Nard did this with two trampolines on the stage of the Amarillo Little Theater. As a promotion for his school and to drum up business he came to a 7th grade Valentines dance at Austin Junior High School and did an exhibition with two of his students. After finding out about Nards school Ronnie convinced his parents to let him sign up for lessons. Nard was his coach (teacher) all the way through high school until he attended the University of Michigan on a scholarship. At that time Ron's competitive teammates in Amarillo were **Charles Rittenberry, Joe Tim Way, Johnnie Hersh, Bill O'Brien, Ann Bynum and Nards daughter Vicki,**

There were other students at the trampoline school as well but these are the ones whom Ron remembers competing with at meets around Texas. Johnny Hamilton was a competitor at the Maverick Club at this time, also.

Nard moved his school to a warehouse behind a drug store on Washington Street with a few more trampolines and from there in

33

the summer of 1954 built the very first trampoline school in the U.S. It's is still there today. (This facility is now All American Gymnastics owned and run by Tim Hall (a former Maverick). During these early years Nards competed against the Maverick Club. As a team they traveled to Fort Worth, Dallas and Austin for Southwest A.A.U. meets.

Who were Ron's heros? Well, certainly Nard! Ron met Larry Griswold for the first time at the trampoline school when Larry was passing through Amarillo. That stuck in his mind since Ron had seen him doing his act on the Ed Sullivan show and thought that was the greatest thing in the world. George Nissen (of course), who he first met in Cedar Rapids on his way to the 1955 Pan American Games. Ron wanted to see the tryouts with Joe Tim. Joe Tim had hoped to make the team. Ron went along for the experience and met George Nissen which was wonderful, Who would have thought at the age of 14 Ron would work for the Nissen Corporation his entire adult life and marry Nissen's wonderful daughter, Dagmar. (She was 4 when they first met in Cedar Rapids)

Ron declares his greatest accomplishments in trampoline competition were winning the 1956 & 59 National AAU championships as well as the 1959 Pan American Games Championship. (Interesting fact: the 1954,1955 & 1956 National AAU Championships was won by Robert Elliott and me, three years running from Amarillo.)

Ron's greatest memories during the competitive years was meeting the other competitors at different meets and developing friendships that even today are still there. George Hery, Gary

Erwin, Steve Johnson, Tom Gomph, Dick Kimball among numerous others were his competitors.

Ron at Nards gym early 1950's.

http://www.trampolinepundit.com/more-notable-vintage-clips/

The great Pyramid Caper
http://hadtrampolinedidtravel.blogspot.com/2013/05/part-1-lets-go-to-egypt.html

Ron placed third the World Professional Trampoline Championships in 1956 and again in 1959. Ron married Dagmar Nissen (George Nissens' daughter).

Outside of George Nissen; Ron and Dagmar have been instrumental in the development of trampoline to it's becoming an Olympic Sport in the World today.

And he's an Amarillo boy!

Ron and Dagmar Munn

Johnny Hamilton

and the 60's

John Hamilton, Louisville, Kentucky
SW AAU Trampoline Champion - 1959,
Big Ten Trampoline Co-Champion - 1964,
NCAA Trampoline Runnerup - 1964,
1965 World Pro Trampoline Ranking - 8

Johnny began competitive tumbling and trampoline at the age of 10 in 1953 with the Maverick Boys Club in Amarillo. He first competed in floor exercise on a wooden floor and rope climb (which is no longer an event), at the Maverick Club. As a freshman, he won the Jr. Olympic Championships and was in the top five in his sophomore and junior year at the AAU Nationals in tumbling. Johnny attended the University of Michigan on a gymnastics scholarship where he was Big 10 Champion, 2nd at the NCAA Championships and was a NCAA All American. Johnny also placed 4th at the 1967 World Professional Championships.

Johnny was a very successful gymnast at Michigan. Johnny has owned and directed a private gym clubs in Levelland, Texas, Lubbock Texas, and Altus, Oklahoma. He has coached at schools throughout Kentucky, Indiana, and Texas. He also taught the Physical Education Majors gymnastics course at Texas Tech while he worked on his Masters degree. One of Johnny's gymnasts, Kelly Garrison, competed in several Olympic Games for the United States. Numerous athletes of his have competed on the national level. Many of his former gymnasts own and direct their own gym clubs. **Wayne Downing, owner of Talent Plus in Lubbock, Texas** is one of his most cherished former students. *He walked into my gym wanting to learn to flip and now is an internationally recognized coach.*

LtoR: Gary Ewin, George Hery, Ronnie Munn, Johnny
Hamilton bottom George Nissen

Johnny is my cousin and has always been someone I admired
and looked up to as a role model. His dad is directly
responsible for forcing me to learn a double back flip. That
helped me overcome my fears and become a successful
gymnast. Johnny was the Head Cheerleader for Michigan
during the Rose Bowl one year

Chapter 5

DAVID JACOBS AND THE 1960'S

STATS CHAMPIONS - TROPHYS WON HOUSTON DEC 28 1960

Tommy Russ/David Jacobs/Kenny Vinyard/ Phillip Garcia

David Jacobs

David started out at the Maverick Club. He was an outstanding
tumbler and beautiful to watch on floor exercise and trampoline.
When I was young my mom would give David a ride home from
the Club. He lived on the North side like we did. David went to
Palo Duro High School my old Alma Mater. Around 1965 David
made the transition over to Nards to get specialized training.

39

Nard always told us a story of David complaining about the noise in the gym while he was doing his routine. Nard being Nard had a cure for that one. He had David do his routine while the kids ran across the tramp yelling. David never lost concentration after that day. David went on to become one the most successful Maverick/Nard products.

In 1967 he won the NCAA on floor for Michigan and placed second in 1969. He won the NCAA trampoline Title in 1967 and 1969 and Placed Second in 1968.

Later in 1967 David won the world Trampoline Championships in London, England and won it again in 1968 in Amersfoort, Netherlands.

David has been Inducted into the World Acrobatic Hall of Fame

Kenny Vinyard

Kenny was a powerhouse of a tumbler and on trampoline. He had really strong legs and could bound and jump all day long. His favorite in tumbling was to do five bounding back flips with a punch front out. Kenny competed a punch front full to a punch front, front roll, front flip, front roll, front flip. On trampoline he was the first person I ever saw do a half-in, half-out. I later copied his style on trampoline. Kenny won many SWAAU Championships on tumbling and trampoline. In 1964 he went to Kings Point Long Island in 1964 for the National AAU Championships and placed third. Ann Bynum from Nards competed at that championships too.

As Kenny got into his high school years he became a very

powerful place kicker for Amarillo High School. He once kicked a fifty yard plus field goal in a game. I think he set the National Place Kicking distance for high school. Kenny went on to Texas Tech and became an All American football player. He is in the Texas Tech Hall of Fame for his kicking. Kenny was drafted by Green Bay with Donnie Anderson. He ended up playing a full year for the Atlanta Falcons.

Kenny after football learned to be a gymnastics coach and won many honors in Texas for his coaching ability.

Ann Bynum

Ann was a national competitor from Nards. She competed at the AAU National Championships in Kings Point Long Island in 1964.

Ann won competitions around Texas, Oklahoma and New Mexico.

Vicki Cazzell

Vicki is Nard's daughter. You might say Vicki was born into the sport. She was always at the gym. Vicki competed through the Southwest.

Vicki married Tim Joe Way and they had a daughter Kimie. Nard was really proud of Vicki and her daughter. He got the privilege of seeing both his daughter and granddaughter enjoy the sport of Trampoline and Tumbling.

Vicki became a very accomplished coach. She and I taught together during my time at Nards. Vicki would run interference between Nard, Sis and I. The kids loved Vicki and she had a major influence on thousands of young athletes.

CHAPTER 6

My Generation

My generation was composed of Richard Womack, Odess Lovin, Johnny Plant, George Dodgen, Roy Smith, Ronnie Webb, Johnny Cobb, Roger Hudson, Jerry Strickland, Steve McFarland, Vance Hall, Linda Shepard, Kathy Dodgen and Shannon Bennett.

Steve McFarland was a Maverick who went to Nard's later. Jerry, Shannon, Vance and Linda were pure Nard products.

Richard (Tex) Womack was a very talented

young tumbler and trampoliner at the Maverick Club. He won various SWAAU Championships. He went to Odessa College and was my roommate. Richard was an All Around gymnast. He became a NJCAA All American in All Around, and Vaulting. After Odessa he went to Tucson and University of Arizona.

Richard has coached National Elite Gymnasts in artistic gymnastics, trampoline, tumbling and double mini-tramp. Richard has coached many International Athletes. He is one of only a few coaches to earn the Master of Sports award from USA Gymnastics for Double Mini Trampoline. Richard has been named Team Coach for International Competition for USA Tumbling and Trampoline in Double Mini trampoline. At this time Richard is still coaching Elite Athletes in Omaha.

Ronnie Webb, Pat Hamilton, Richard Womack, Mike Shanks and Roger Hudson competed in the 60's for the Maverick Club. Later we all went to Odessa College on Full Athletic Scholarships. Odessa won the NJCAA National championships and all these athletes became All American Gymnasts. Odess went to Oklahoma as a Freshman.

Ronnie Webb, Johnny Cobb, Odess Lovin, George Dodgen, Johnny Plant and I competed in the AAU National Gymnastics Championships in Bartlesville, Oklahoma 1966, Natchitoches Louisiana 1967 and the Olympic Trials in Los Angeles in 1968. Odess competed in the Nationals in Atlanta in 1967. Odess placed second in tumbling in 1966, 1967 and 1968.

Johnny Cobb dropped gymnastics for wrestling after high school. He was Texas State Wrestling Champion. Johnny went to Oklahoma State on a Wrestling Scholarship. Johnny has become wrestling legend in Amarillo, throughout Texas and the World. Johnny coached Brandon Slay who became the 2000 Olympic Gold Medal Champion in wrestling.

Johnny was the wrestling coach at Tascosa High School and developed a wrestling program for the Maverick Club that has produced many outstanding wrestlers like Brandon Slay, Steve Nelson , Scott Tankersley (Scott has coached 7 UIL State Champions), Johnny finished his wrestling by starting and developing the wrestling program at Wayland Baptist.

Johnny Cobb became the first-ever coach of the new men's and women's wrestling program at Wayland Baptist. Johnny was a two-time Texas High School Coach of the Year while at Tascosa High School, in Amarillo. He is a member of the Texas Wrestling Ring of Honor and the Texas chapter of the National Wrestling Hall of Fame in Stillwater, Okla.

Johnny was a three-time District Champion at Tascosa High School in the mid-60's, losing only one high school match in three years of competition. He went on to wrestle at Oklahoma State University until injuries put a premature end to his collegiate wrestling career.

Johnny is one of the founding members of the Panhandle Amateur Wrestling Association, he also founded the first kid's wrestling program in the Panhandle of Texas at the Maverick Boys Club in 1971. His teams won both elementary and junior high team state championships titles and over 50 elementary and junior high individual state titles.

Johnny took over as wrestling coach for both the boy's and girl's programs at Tascosa High School in 1988. Between 1990 and his retirement in 2008,

Johnny's teams won three state championships and finished in the top ten 15 times. Twenty-one Tascosa High wrestlers earned individual state titles under Cobb's tutelage, 28 were national qualifiers, and one, Brandon Slay, won the 2000 Olympic Gold Medal.

Odess Lovin

Odess was the most flexible Maverick ever. He was one of the most talented of my age group. Odess placed second in tumbling at the National AAU Championships in Natchitoches , Atlanta and Los Angeles. Odess went to Palo Duro High School with me. Odess was the first of my age group to try and learn a double back flip. We all lined up and his dad spotted him using the traveling tumbling belt. He ran down the mat threw the double and landed right on his head. His dad pulled the rope a fraction too late. After he got out of the hospital he really did well. He was one of the first to alternate double full twists on tumbling.

After high school Odess went to Oklahoma on a full athletic scholarship. He won the NCAA Championships on Floor in 1971 and 1972. He was named a NCAA All American on Floor Exercise in 1971 and 1972

Ronnie Webb

Ronnie was the first Maverick to go to Odessa College. He was Texas Collegiate Champion in All Around and Vaulting. Ronnie helped pace the Odessa Team as its Captain to a Second Place finish in the first NJCAA Championships in Miami Florida. Ronnie went to Oklahoma on a full athletic scholarship. He later won the Big Eight in Vaulting.

Jerry Strickland

Jerry was a tough competitor from Nards. When we would go to meets he usually won on trampoline. He tried to compete with us on tumbling but couldn't quite catch us. I always said we were as good on tumbling as he was on trampoline but second place is OK. Mr. Dykeman always told us if we couldn't win then make sure the winner has to set the record. Jerry set the record.

Jerry became an outstanding coach. He has coached National Champions and elite trampoline and double mini-tramp champions for well over 40 years. Jerry is currently coaching elite gymnasts in Austin, Texas.

When Jerry came out of high school he went to Oklahoma on an athletic scholarship. That was 1968 the year the NCAA eliminated trampoline from its competitions. Bad luck for Jerry. Jerry finally retired from competition because of a severe knee injury.

Jerry and Odess Lovin started a gymnastics school in Amarillo. They called it the O-JAYS. Odess left and became a CFO at one of the feedlots in the Panhandle. Jerry continued coaching at the gym. I bought Jerry's operation and Jerry moved to Austin. The economy took a dive in the Panhandle and I sold the gym and moved to Victoria, Texas to work for Cindy Burkett-Seerden and Gymagic.

Jerry has been able to accomplish many wonderful things in Austin. He has coached many athletes in trampoline, tumbling and double mini-tramp to the National and Elite Levels and we continue to be close friends.

Linda Shepard

"Here are a couple of hard-and-fast Nard Rules:

Never, ever say "can't." Violating this rule got you a bonk on the head with his hand-- *the hand where he wore a large (hard) ring.*

We were not allowed to complain about the judging. The solution was to be so much better than the other competitors that the judges couldn't dispute it.

Nard was all about helping kids, and it didn't matter what team they were on. Often during warm-ups, I heard him giving helpful tips to my competitors -- ones that weren't on our team!

I remember being shocked when we had to start wearing leotards. The clinging things were super tight, showed a lot of skin, and were alarmingly revealing and risqué for the modest teen I was at the time. I eventually got over it (boy, did I), but in the first meet (along with the all black leotard) I chose to also wear black ballet tights to cover my long legs. That earned me the nickname (from some of my less modest friends who shall remain nameless) of Spider Woman.

While I'm speaking of leotards, allow me to point out that in those pioneer days, we didn't have the cute, colorful ones with flattering cuts that they have today. We considered ourselves trendsetters the year we switched to all-white. They still weren't the high-cuts that kept your legs from looking like tree trunks, but they were a small improvement.

The fact that these leotards showed every curve, lump, and defect led to a very comical incident at one of the meets. I swear I am not the star in this story, but one of the not-yet-developed trampolinists had padded her bra with toilet paper to add a bit of shape. During her routine, long ribbons of tissue trailed out of the top of her leotard as she flipped and twisted her way through 10 tricks.

I'm pretty sure this next unfortunate incident happened to Shannon Bennett. It was a rule in the Tumbling world long hair on boys was not allowed. There was no way Shannon was going to chop of his precious locks, so he tried to beat the system with a wig. Yep. When he finished his run, there in the middle of the tumbling mat was what appeared to be a dead animal of some sort.

Kathy Dodgen and I qualified for the 1969 Nationals in Sarasota, Florida. Because of either the expense or some scheduling conflict (I don't recall the reason), Nard wasn't going to go with us-- nor was any adult. It was just going to be us; two girls and the 4 boys

47

on the team. (*Understand that I was raised in a very proper family, so when my parents found out that the plan was for the six of us fly cross-country for several days unaccompanied, it was a No Go. That just wasn't done.*) How would it look? Blah, blah, blah. No way was I going to be allowed to go. Long story short, Newt Loken, at the time a professor at the University Michigan, agreed to meet up with us in Sarasota and act as our chaperone. Notice that in the newspaper article about the meet, that important trip detail was included. As it played out, I think Newt waved to us from across the gym once and that was extent of his supervision. But the important thing is that I was there to wave back, and my Mom and Dad weren't ostracized for being bad parents.

I wish I could think of some Sis stories. She was a character in her own right and often said things that were not run through a filter before the words came out of her mouth. It was one of the things that made her so much fun and such a hoot to be around. She also was much loved.

I dearly loved both Nard and Sis. They and my exposure to the teammates I had at Nards made me tougher. Much of the success I've had in life I can trace back to my experiences at their gym both as a competitor and as a coach. All the coaching I did for them helped tremendously in the raising of our three kids."

Johnny Cobb

Johnny was an outstanding tumbler in the early sixties. He could do flip-flops and bounders all day long. Johnny was very talented in gymnastics but more talented in wrestling. Johnny had only one defeat in his entire high school wrestling career. Johnny was given athletic scholarship offers in gymnastics but decided to follow his wrestling goals. He went to Oklahoma State on Athletic Scholarship. He made the right decision.

Johnny started a wrestling program at the Maverick. His program produced many talented boys and girls in wrestling.

Johnny was the wrestling coach at Tascosa High School that won many state titles for boys and girls. Johnny was inducted into the **Panhandle Sports Hall of Fame in 2018.**

Johnny coached Brandon Slay the Olympic Gold Medal winner in wrestling in the 2000 Olympic Games. Brandon won three State Titles under Johnny Cobb and went to the University of Pennsylvania where he was a two time All-American and two time runner-up in the NCAA Championships.

Wayland Baptist College wanted a wrestling program so they hired Johnny to develop the program.

While at Wayland Johnny coached 2017 U.S. World Team member Tamyra Mensah.

Johnny has been a top coach at all levels in Texas and is active in USA Wrestling on the national level.

Johnny is instrumental in the development of age group wrestling through Texas and the United States.

Steve McFarland

Steve started diving in Phoenix at age 10. He moved to Texas. There his dad enrolled him in the Maverick Club to learn to tumble and trampoline. Steve was very talented and had some of the best form I ever saw. He was quite accomplished and won many awards while at the Club. His dad moved him over to Nard and he became team mates with Jerry Strickland and Linda Shepard. He got to watch David Jacobs while he was learning. He learned well. His form was beautiful. I had to compete with Jerry and him at every meet. We three along with Bobby Sargent from Austin and Richard Womack and Roger Hudson from the Maverick Club usually made the top six at the competitions in Midland, Oklahoma City, Dallas Athletic Club Dallas Sokol, the Houston JCC and Texas City. Of course it was always a tough competition at the Maverick Club Meet held the first week in March to celebrate Mr. Dykeman's birthday. The one that won was usually Bobby Sargent, Jerry Strickland, Roger Hudson or Steve McFarland, unless they fell. (Which happened a lot.) I went my first year without winning a medal until the Texas City Meet when everyone fell but me. I was so proud!

Steve almost chose trampoline over diving, but the NCAA dropped the sport. After two years at the University of Texas, he transferred to the University of Miami, diving for Tom Gompf and winning two AAU National Championships on platform, 1973, 1974 and two bronze medals at the World University Games in 1974 in springboard and platform. He performed in comedy shows and became an athlete representative in diving's governing body, USA Diving.

His passion for the sport took him in many directions. He succeeded Tom as coach at Miami, where Steve worked with legendries Greg Louganis and Phil Boggs and also coached four NCAA All-Americans (1977-1984). He was asked to be a television communicator for diving, broadcasting for NBC at the 1988 and 1992 Olympics (where the Pay Per View broadcast was the first complete live coverage of an Olympic Games), ESPN (1993-1996), Turner Broadcast Sports (1989-1992) and broadcasts with Outdoor Life Network, Prime Network FINA Video and HDTV Net. He was producer and narrator of "100 Years of

Diving Success" shown at the successful 2004 U.S. Olympic Diving Trials, which he hosted and conducted.

As a volunteer and administrator, Steve has been Vice President of USA Diving (1985-1993, 2004-present) and served as President (1994-1998). He has been an Olympic Diving Judge at the 200 Sydney and 2004 Athens Games.

Steve was USA Diving Age Group Coach of the Year (1980).

Mike Shanks

Mike competed All Around in gymnastics. He accepted a full athletic scholarship to Odessa College along with Roger Hudson. Mike was a member of the National Champion NJCAA Team in 1971. After Odessa Mike moved on to North Texas State here he placed in the Texas Collegiate Championships. After college Mike became a stuntman for movies with many credits to his name.

Roger Hudson

Roger was a super star as a young man. He was outstanding on trampoline and tumbling. He made the Trip to be in the halftime show at the Rose Bowl with the Maverick Club.

Roger went to my high school at Palo Duro High along with Odess Lovin.

In 1968 Roger, Odess and I won second place at the Texas High School Championships in Division II at LD Bell High School. Roger received a full athletic scholarship at Odessa College and won first Place in 1969 and 1970 in floor exercise and became a NJCAA All-American. He placed on Vaulting too. Roger followed me to L.S.U. New Orleans on full athletic scholarship after Odessa. He broke his ankle on trampoline and it ended his carrer.

Johnny Plant

Johnny Plant and Roger Hudson were two of the best young tumblers in Texas. They were doing double full twists by seven years old. All the young tumblers at the Maverick Club could do full twists and most could do doubles, except for me. I learned my full and double when I was 15. I was a little slow. Johnny could throw a triple full on floor in the 1950's.

Johnny's' career ended when he was 12. He he jumped over a ledge at Palo Duro Canyon and fell 30 feet breaking his ankle. Johnny went on to become one of the most outstanding hair fashion stylists in the United States. He is known the world over for his talent and innovations.

Roy Smith

Roy was an outstanding young tumbler at the Maverick Club. He won most of the competitions we were in. He was in the 9-10 age group when I was in the 15-18 age group. Roy moved to Dallas when he was in Middle School and didn't pursue his gymnastics training.

Pat Hamilton

I was a slow starter. I finally learned my back handspring when I was 14. I struggled on tumbling but did better on trampoline. By 16 I could throw Full in back out, brani-in-back out, half-in and half-out, front two and three quarter and alternate triple full twists at the end of my trampoline routine.

I went to Odessa College with Richard Womack in 1968. I won the NCJAA Championships on Floor Exercise and Trampoline and became a Collegiate All American. I went to L.S.U. at New Orleans on full athletic scholarship. I had offers from CSU, Indiana, Indiana State University and L.S.U. New Orleans. I chose New Orleans because of the city of New Orleans and the coach Lloyd Huval. Roger Hudson followed me to Louisiana the next year.

When I returned from college, I worked at the Maverick Club on work study from West Texas State. I was married and had a young son, Ronnie. Nard came to me and asked me to coach for him. He offered me $ 600 a month. I needed the money so I moved over to work for him. I felt like a traitor but I had to support my family.

While at Nard's, I learned a lot about life. Nard was a business man and knew the tricks of the business world. At one time Nard was part owner of the American Restaurant in Amarillo. My uncles, Jimmy and Kenneth, worked for him before going into the Marines and fighting in the Korean War in 1951. Both lost their lives over there. Jimmy earning the Silver Star and Kenneth the Bronze Star.

Nard taught me to be a coach. I watched him and learned. I was able to combine what Mr. Dykeman had taught me and what Nard taught me to go on and coach my entire life. Tim Hall followed in my footsteps and left the Club to work for Nard. Tim eventually was able to purchase Nard's and it became All American Gymnastics. Tim has coached many National and World Champions from Amarillo.

I worked at the Maverick Club and then Nards. I learned so much from Ralph Dykeman and Nard Cazzell that it set the pattern of my life. (*I actually lived in Nards Gym for a little while back in 1973.*)

I moved to El Paso and worked for the YMCA there. I coached my first Elite Gymnasts in El Paso. Pam Lee and Kim Strauss. Pam qualified for the Championships of the USA. She competed in the Mardi Gras Invitational at L.S.U. and placed second in All Around behind Kathy Johnson. Kim qualified for the National Championships and became a high school and collegiate All American. I became the Head Gymnastics Coach for Women at the University of Texas El Paso. I recruited Olympian Teresa Diaz Sandi from Mexico to be on the team. I had one of the first college programs to offer scholarships in Texas for gymnastics.

From El Paso I moved to Coach at the National Training Center in Arlington, Texas. While in Arlington I helped with the World

Gymnastics Championships in 1979. I coached at Arlington Gymnastics School in a competition against the Japanese National Junior Team. Two of the girls I coached qualified for the USGF National Championships. Kim Miner and Kim Strauss.

I was fortunate to coach athletes that received full athletic scholarships to Stanford, Kentucky, Centenary, New Mexico, and Oklahoma. I've coached over twenty high school All Americans and several Collegiate All Americans during my coaching career.

In 1980 I coached at McCallum High School in Austin, Texas. My boy's team won the Texas High School Championships for Division Two. I coached at various gyms during the 80's.

In 1983 while coaching at the University of Gymnastics in Plano Texas I took a group of 10 girls to a competition in Budapest Hungry and we watched the 1983 World Gymnastics Championships.

In 1985 I moved back to Amarillo and worked for Jerry Strickland. I purchased the gym from Jerry so he could move to Austin. Later I sold the gym and moved to Victoria, Texas. Amarillo was hit hard by the economic downturn in the late 80's.

In 1994 I coached for Cindy Burkett-Seerden at Gymagic in Victoria, Texas. I told her about how much fun she could have doing tumbling and trampoline. Cindy decided to transform her gym into a tumbling and trampoline center. She did it the right way and hired some of the very best to teach her how to compete in the sport. She is now one of the premiere and most respected coaches in the United States.

While in Victoria I also coached middle school boys in football, basketball and track. While coaching track a boy hit me in the head with a pole-vaulting pole (by accident) and broke my neck. My gymnastics career came to an end at that time.

I took the energy, passion and drive I had with gymnastics to learn educational technology. I got started on the ground floor of educational technology. I became an Apple Distinguished Educator and a Computerworld Smithsonian Laureate. My program was named one of the top programs in America. I have been published many times with articles on Technology Integration Into the Academic Curriculum. I was awarded a grant from Harvard University in Educational Technology and completed 15 hours of Graduate work. I attended the Stanford Institute of Technology Leadership and I lectured at National Association for Curriculum Development and Magnet Schools of America.

The Gymnastics Association of Texas honored me with the **Service to Youth Award (2002)** and **The Gymnastics Heritage Award in 2004.**

I started coaching in the Rio Grande Valley in Harlingen, Texas in 2013. I wanted to see if I could do it without spotting. (I couldn't spot because of my neck injury) I coached Trampoline, Tumbling and Double Mini Trampoline. With hard work and talented kids I was able to coach several athletes into the USA Gymnastics National Age Group Tumbling and Trampoline Championships. I retired in 2018 and went fishing at South Padre Island. I live in Port Isabel, Texas on an island.

I love the sport of gymnastics and the people with whom I have been involved. It has made my life full. I have great memories of the wonderful people I have met through this sport

Billy Bob Taylor

Billy Bob competed on the team with Tim Hall, Gary Hedrick, Tay Carter, Bruce Carter, Scott Elliott and Steve Elliott at the Maverick Club.

Billy Bob has distinguished himself by starting and operating The Maverick Club Gymnastics Program in Charleston, West Virginia. Billy Bob has produced Elite and Champion gymnasts for over thirty years and he's still going strong!

Kathy Dodgen

Kathy's brother George and I were best friends. Kathy would come to the Maverick Club and hang around while we all worked on tumbling and trampoline. Well she caught the bug and wanted to do it too.

Kathy learned a few things at the Club and worked with all the guys and Steve Elliott's dad, Robert. Since she was a girl she had little time to work at the Boys club. Kathy's family finally raked up enough funds to allow Kathy to go to Nard's for training.

Kathy won competitions throughout Texas, New Mexico and Oklahoma. She competed at the Southwest AAU and at the National AAU Championships.

Kathy received an athletic scholarship at the prestigious University of Southwestern Louisiana with Jeff Hennessy. Jeff Hennessy was one of the most important coaches in the development of Trampoline. Jeff wrote the book on trampoline, literally! Early in Kathy's career at Southwestern she fell and broke her ankle. That ended her trampoline pursuit.

Amarillo College Gymnastics

In 1972 Nard had a brilliant idea. Nard was having difficulty getting qualified coaches to work at his gym. I was the Head Gymnastics Coach but we needed class teachers. Nard worked a deal with Amarillo College to start a Women's gymnastics Team. Winnie Montgomery was named the Coach of the Team. Girls included on the team were Leslie Elston, Ann Notestin, Cindy Potts, Cheryl Medley, Susanne Blackwell and Patti Taylor. *Yes this is the same Cheryl Jarrett that has gone on to run the Membership of USA Gymnastics and owner of Capitol Gymnastics in Austin with her husband Jimbo!*

The girls competed for Amarillo College and worked at the gym teaching classes at Nards. Sis (Nards wife), Linda Shepard and I were put in charge of working with the girls in the gym and Winnie worked with them at Amarillo College.

Front Row Cheryl Medley, Susanne Blakwell, Lerslie Elston and Patti Taylor

Back Row Ann Notestine, Coach Winnie Montgomery, and Cindy Potts   *Photo Amarillo Glob News*

Chapter 7

Tim Hall

Tim started gymnastics at age 6 in 1967 at the Maverick Boys Club under Ralph Dykeman. His first competition was at age 8 in 1969 in All Around Gymnastics, tumbling and trampoline. By the time Tim was 14, he was competing throughout Texas. He even started helping out with the coaching of the boys at the Club.

By the time Tim was 18, gymnastics had died out at the Maverick Club so he moved over to Nards. (He found out that he had to make a living and Nard actually paid!)

While at Nards Tim learned to coach Women's Artistic Gymnastics and learned a lot more about coaching Trampoline and Tumbling. Tim retired from competition at age 23 and placed all his energy into becoming an outstanding coach.

Tim has coached such outstanding athletes as Chad Fox at 9 years old, Jon Beck at age 7, Kim Joe (Nard's granddaughter), and many, many more talented athletes. Time has coached so many state, national and International Champions it would be too vast to list here.

While coaching at Nards Tim helped build the STTA in Texas. In 1985 Tim purchased Nards and renamed it All American Gymnastics. All American has produced more than 500 state Champions, 200 National Champions and 10 world and International Champions. Tim has received Texas Coach of the Year twelve times and has been honored as National coach of the

Year.

Tim has been honored many times and has represented the United States as Team Coach on numerous occasions throughout the world. Tim has coached 3 different athletes into the Acrobatic Hall of fame and the USA Gymnastics Hall of fame.

Tim had a helping hand in getting Trampoline into the Olympic Games. All American (Nards) has been taking Amarillo's youth to a higher level for over 62 years. Recently Tim has had the honor of coaching Shaylee Dunivan into the 2016 Olympic Games in Rio as an alternate to the USA women's trampoline Team.

Tim has been inducted into the World Acrobatic Society Hall of Fame in 2018.

Chapter 8
Chad Fox-Jon Beck-Byron Smith

Chad Fox

Chad didn't really have any choice in becoming great in the trampoline and tumbling world. Of course he had Nard and all that behind him but few know about his mom Polly and sister Lisa. Polly was a coach with me at Nards in the early 70's. We taught all the classes. Polly wasn't just a coach she was like a sister to me and Sis Cazzell. Polly was a team mom to the girls. She coached them and loved them all. Lisa (Chad's sister) was one of the talented girls on the team. Chad's step-dad was Roy McCoy our local Weatherman and News Reporter.

Chad came to the gym and he just had to become good. He had so much talent.

When I worked with Chad he was just a little munchkin being a gym "rat". He picked up skills easily. Nard would love to show him off with the tumbling he could do.

I enjoyed working with him, Cliffie Lewellan and Bill Miller on gymnastics skills. There were others like Kip Fraiser, Jennifer Barbie, Joni Miller, Jennifer Miller and Susan Canode that made up a very talented team at Nards.

Chad was good but didn't become great until well after I left Nard's. Chad is a graduate of Palo Duro High School. David Jacobs, Roger Hudson, Odess Lovin and I all went to PD. That's

because we all lived on the North Side of Amarillo.

By the age of 19, Chad had won 14 national titles in trampoline, mini-trampoline, and tumbling.

Chad went on to the University of New Mexico for college to work under World-renowned coach Rusty Mitchell. Chad became the first male gymnast to win four individual titles on the same apparatus when he won titles in the vault from 1986-1989. In 1987, Fox added another national title in floor exercise to the vault, becoming the first UNM gymnast to win two national championships in the same year.

When Chad came out of high school he had many offers to go to school in diving on athletic scholarship. He chose to go to New Mexico instead. He had to try out for the team and didn't receive a scholarship. He made the team and then made history. He won the NCAA in vaulting his freshman year and dominated for the next three years winning each year he was in school. Chad also managed to win the NCAA title in Floor Exercise and Vaulting in 1987.

When I was at my gym in Amarillo in the late 80's. Chad called me and asked if I would spot him on a double layout on floor. I thought he could already do it but I wanted to help so I said OK. Chad and Jon Beck showed up at my gym.

I stood on the floor and waited. Chad ran across the gym which was only as wide as a floor mat and maybe 10 extra feet. I had never seen such power from a tumbler. It was beautiful. Of course he didn't need me at all. That's the point. I'm sure Nard sent him over to prove how good Chad was. The trick was on Nard because I already knew Chad and Jon were outstanding. Nard loved playing little tricks from time to time.

Chad was the 173rd Member Inducted Panhandle Sports Hall Of Fame. Chad had unprecedented accomplishments in the world of trampoline, tumbling, diving, and later gymnastics. In his mid-teens, Fox was winning gold and silver medals in Japan and power tumbling in Paris while competing elsewhere internationally on an annual basis in different acrobatic disciplines.

By age 19, Fox had won 14 national titles in trampoline, mini-trampoline, tumbling and artistic gymnastics, and three world tumbling titles. At the University of New Mexico, Fox made NCAA history as the first male gymnast to win four individual titles on the same apparatus when he won titles in the vault from 1986-89. In 1987, Fox also added an NCAA title in floor exercise to the vault, becoming the first UNM gymnast to win two national championships in the same year.

Jon Beck

Jon starts the group that I really had very little contact with. This group was very accomplished.

Jon won Silver in Tumbling at World's in Essen Germany in 1990. He took the Gold Medal in 1992 in Auckland, New Zealand.

Jon was inducted into the World Acrobatic Society Hall of Fame in 2009

Jon was inducted into the United States Gymnastics Hall of Fame in 2012.

Jon Beck, Steve Elliott, Tim Hall

Byron Smith

Byron was the young guy at Nards coming in right after Chad Fox and Jon Beck. Here is a list of his accomplishments:

- 1998, 2000 Synchro National Champion with Karl Heger
- 1998 National Championships, St. Paul, Minn.; 1st-Synchro, 3rd-Trampoline
- 1999 National Championships, Anaheim, Calif.; 2nd-Synchro, 4th-Trampoline
- 1999 World Championships Team Double Mini Gold Medalist
- 1999 World Championships, Sun City, South Africa; 1st-Team Double Mini
- National Competition

- 2000 National Championships, St. Louis, Mo.; 1st-Synchro, 3rd-Trampoline
- 2001 National Championships, San Antonio, Texas; 3rd-Trampoline
- 2002 Winter Classic, Indianapolis, IN; 3rd-Trampoline, 7th-Double Mini

Byron is a coach for Air Extreme in Lubbock, Texas and he has coached many National Competitors.

Byron has been inducted into the United States Acrobatic Gymnastics Hall of Fame.

Chapter 9

Steve Elliott, Billy Bob Taylor, Scott Elliott, Gary Hedrick

Steve is the son of Robert Elliott. Robert won the United States and Canadian Trampoline Title in 1954 and 1955. Steve started at the Maverick Club as soon as his dad could get him in.

I was coaching at the Club when Steve began. He was so talented. He could out tumble most of us by the time he was six. I was working with him one day and he did a Loop into a back flip off the pommel horse. Steve was talented in everything but especially trampoline and tumbling.

Steve is the most accomplished athlete to come out of the Club. He won eight World Tumbling and Double Mini Trampoline Championships. In 1980 and 1982, Steve won the NCAA in Floor Exercise and helped pace Nebraska to the National Team Championships. Steve also won the NCAA Vaulting Championships in 1982.

It's interesting to note that Steve went to Nebraska on a diving scholarship not a gymnastics scholarship. After college Steve went on to teach at Camp Woodward in Woodward Pennsylvania. Steven coached in Cincinnati where he helped coach Olympian Amanda Borden.

Once I took my team to The University of Utah Gymnastics Camp. A young man on my team was Roger Graham. Roger and Steve were good friends. Steve met us in Salt Lake for the camp. We all went to Michelle Ponds Gym (Daughter of Charlie Pond) to work out. Steve and Roger got into a double mini tramp battle to see what they could do. Each time one would add a flip or a twist the next one would add to it. I have never seen such courage and skill in all my life and at that time I was a member of the Elite Coaches association of the United States. Steve went on to win World Championships and Roger place third.

Scott and Steve Elliott

Scott Elliott

Scott is the son of Robert and brother of Steve and he is a very accomplished athlete. Scott was a tumbler at the Maverick Club. He competed at the World Age Group Games in Kanazawa, Japan in 1984. Scott went on to the University of Mississippi and became a cheerleader. Scott became a leader in the Universal Cheerleading Association (UCA). Scott spends most of his time these days running projects and functions for the Special Olympics and other organizations for disabled and the disadvantaged. Scott has spearheaded many safety initiatives in cheerleading and helped launch the American Association of Cheerleading Coaches and Administration (AACCA)

Gary Hedrick

Gary started off tumbling at the Maverick Club in 1967. He started Coaching at the Maverick Club in 1976. He stayed at the Maverick Club until 1981.

From 1981 to 1983 he coached Gymnastics at the Amarillo School of Gymnastics with Jerry Strickland (Jerry lives in Austin). From 1983 to 1985 he coached at Gymnastics of Dallas with Kenny Vinyard. From 1983 to 1984 Gary was with the Texas Armadillo Association.

The Amarillo Armadillo he travelled with the Texas Armadillo Association to promote the Texas 9 banded Armadillo with a 30-foot plexi-glass racetrack and 8 live armadillos and had armadillo races. The Texas Armadillo Association led to Gary getting a job with the American Eagles High Diving Team. Gary was also a cliff diver for 15 years and moved to Hong Kong for 4 months and Taiwan for 3 months. He was with the American Eagles Professional High Diving Platform Company. He was the feature comedian for the Comedy Trampoline show and also one of the divers. They did regular diving, comedy diving and the HIGH Dive (100 feet off of towers)!

From 1990 to 1993 Gary coached Tumbling, Trampoline, and Double-Mini at Top of Texas Tumblers in Lubbock, TX. From 2000 to 2005 he coached at Metroplex Gymnastics of Dallas. He coached at the Palaestra of Dallas coaching tumbling, trampoline, and double-mini tramp.

His accomplishments and awards:
- Nine Time National Tumbling and Trampoline, and Double-Mini Trampoline

- Two times 3rd in World Championships in Tumbling, 1st in Double-Mini
- Three time All-American
- Three time U.S. Tumbling and Trampoline Team Member
- Three time Athlete of the Year in West Texas
- Gary has also been a "CHARACTER" most of his life. Costume characters!
- He was the Amarillo Armadillo off and on for 6 years.
- SKIDS the Penguin (Christmas Funds for Children in Atlanta, Georgia). He was Dr. Well-Bee for the Scottish Rites Hospital in Atlanta, Georgia.
- Mama Hawk for the Atlanta Hawks NBA Basketball Team in Atlanta.
- The Tasmanian Devil which was the Official Mascot for the 1998 Goodwill Games in New York, New York.

His most famous character was Wildcat Willie from   World Championship Wrestling working out of Atlanta, Georgia.

- Jeeves the Butler for Lord Steven Regal and Dave Taylor's tag-team of the Blue-Bloods.   WCW was owned by TBS, (Turner Broadcasting System). Gary said, "Yes, Ted Turner signed my paycheck"! Gary was with TBS and WCW for almost 6 years until World Wrestling Federation (WWF), bought them out. Now WWF is now WWE.
- He worked as Wild Cat Willie for 5 years with the Make-A-Wish Foundation (Atlanta and Orlando). As Wild Cat Willie, he worked with the Scottish Rites Hospitals in Atlanta and all over the US. Wild Cat Willie won the 1st. Scottish Rites Children's Hospital Professional Celebrity Mascot Golf Tournament. (Yes in costume)!
- Last but not least Gary was with the World Famous Bud Light Daredevils. They were a professional Acrobatic Slam-Dunk Show.
- Gary travelled to 12 different countries and performed for

every NBA team, and   over 50 Colleges, and was a Feature
Show on ESPN. On this Feature Show, Gary made the
highlights on George Michaels Sports Machine with a foot
to the face (ouch!). All in all with the Gymnastics,
Costume characters, Diving, Professional Wrestling, and
the Bud Light Daredevils, Gary has performed in front of
or on television for over 2,100,000,000 (2.1 BILLION)

Chapter 10

Shaylee Dunivan

Shaylee started out being coached by Tim Hall at All American Gymnastics. She is a current powerhouse in Trampoline, Double Mini Tram and Synchro Trampoline. Shaylee was the alternate to the Olympic Team that competed in Rio. Shaylee is where I will stop my journal of Amarillo Superstars and leave it to someone else to carry on from this point.

Career Highlights

- **Alternate for the 2016 Olympic Games**
- 2016 U.S. trampoline & synchro champion
- 2016 Pacific Rim trampoline silver medalist
- 2015 U.S. synchro champion
- 2014 U.S. trampoline & synchro silver medalist
- Member of the 2013-15 World Championships Teams
- 2013 U.S. synchro champion and trampoline bronze medalist

Our Competitions 1964-1968

When I was at the Club we had competitions throughout Texas, Oklahoma and New Mexico. Our first competition of the year was always at the YMCA in Midland, Texas. One year we competed trampoline in a handball room. Then we might go to the Oklahoma Twisters in Oklahoma City. With Janie Speaks (Olympics 1964), Debbie Bailey (Pan American Games 1967 Silver Medal on Balance Beam and World Championships 1966), Kathy Carroll (Top15 USA 1967), Debbie Carroll. Mickey Hester, MiMi Quinton, and Coach Nance. From down south was Bobby Sargent. Bobby became a famous stuntman with many, many important credits to his name. The Maverick Club Meet was always around March 4th. (Mr. Dykeman's birthday). Competitions in the early spring would be at Eastern New Mexico State in Portales New Mexico with Garland O'Quinn. We would compete in Dallas at the Dallas SOKOL and the Dallas Athletics Club. Down south was Bill Crenshaw in Austin. Our big competitions were usually held in Dallas at the Southwest AAU Championships. Gymnasts I remember were **Laurie Harris, Patti Dilbeck, JoAnn Camesie, Karla Kelson, Kathy and Debbie Carroll, Janie Speaks, Debbie Bailey, Mimi Quinton, Micki Hester, Tom Cunningham, Bobby Sargent and Marc Yancey.**

World Professional Trampoline Championships 1967
https://www.youtube.com/watch?v=fbQAsF2hxKY

Second Worlds Trampoline Championships

https://www.youtube.com/watch?v=adkaFFvMqu8

World Professional championships 1967

https://www.youtube.com/watch?v=fbQAsF2hxKY

Amarillo Champions

Edsel Buchanan	49, 50, 51	NCAA Champion
Robert Elliott	54, 55	US and Canadian Champion
Ronnie Munn	56, 59	US Championships 1st Place
	1959	Pan American Games Champion
	1965	3rd Place World Pro
	1967	3rd Place World Pro

(Interesting fact...the 1954,1955 & 1956   National AAU Championships was won by Robert Elliott and Ron, three years running from Amarillo.)

Johnny Hamilton	1964	2nd Place NCAA Tramp
	1963	4th Place NCAA Tramp
	1967	4th Place World Professional

		Championships
David Jacobs	1966	Synchro World Champion
	1967	World Champion
	1968	World Champion
	1967	1st NCAA Floor Exercise
Odess Lovin	1971	1st NCAA Floor Exercise
	1972	1st NCAA Floor Exercise
	67, 68, 69	2nd AAU Tumbling
Jon Beck	1988	Trampoline National Champ
	1988 and 1990	Double Mini Tramp National Champion
	1992	Tumbling World Champion
	1988 and 1993	Tumbling National Champion
Steve Elliott	1978, 80, 81, 85	World Tumbling Champion
		NCAA Floor

Chad Fox	1980, 82	Exercise Champion
	1982	NCAA Vaulting Champion
	1983, 86	World Tumbling Champion
	86, 87, 88,89	NCAA Vaulting Champion, 4 years in a row, NCAA Record
Byron Smith	1988	NCAA Floor Exercise
	1999	World Champion Team Trampoline (Sun City, south Africa)
	1998, 2000	National Synchro Champion
	1998	National Champion Syncro
	1999	1st Syncro, 3rd Trampoline
		National Championship 2nd Syncro,

Shaylee Dunavin, Dakota Earnest	2015	4th Trampoline team at World championships National Synchro Champion
	2016	National Synchro
Shaylee Dunivan	2016	National Trampoline Champion
	2016	Alternate to Olympic Games in RIO

ABOUT THE AUTHOR

Pat Hamilton was a member of the Maverick Boys Club gymnastics program from 1956 to 1971. He moved to coach for Nard Cazzell in 1971 through 1973. After Leaving Nards in 1973 he moved to Coach in El Paso Texas. Pat Coached at the YMCA and at the University of Texas El Paso. Pat was the Head Coach for Women at the University of Texas El Paso and awarded athletic scholarships to many Texas athletes. While at UTEP he coached Theresa Diaz Sandie, Olympic Competitor from Mexico.

Pat has coached in Houston, Amarillo, Austin, El Paso, Arlington, Plano, Victoria and Harlingen. Pat received full Athletic Scholarships at Odessa College and Louisiana State University at New Orleans. While at Odessa College Pat won the first National Junior College Championships in Floor Exercise and Trampoline. Pat became a NJCAA All American and was Co-Captain of the National Junior College Championship Team in 1970.

Pat is married and has six children. Mandi (Pat's daughter) competed at the World Age Group Championships and placed third on double mini trampoline. She competed nationally in tumbling and trampoline for Gymagic and Cindy Burkett-Seerden in Victoria, Texas. Pat has had the joy of watching two of his granddaughters (Kaitlyn and Shaylee) compete nationally in trampoline and tumbling and double mini trampoline